by Katie Hart

SCHOOL PUBLISHERS

Cover, ©Alaska Stock; p.3, ©Paul A. Souders/CORBIS; p.4, ©Alaska Stock; p.5, ©Alaska Stock; p.6, ©Alaska Stock; p.8, ©Alaska Stock; p.9, ©Kennan Ward/CORBIS; p.10, ©Paul Souders/Accent Alaska; p.11, ©Alaska Stock; p.12, ©Alaska Stock; p.14, ©Alaska Stock.

Copyright © by Harcourt, Inc.

All rights reserved. No part of this publication may be reproduced or transmitted in any form or by any means, electronic or mechanical, including photocopy, recording, or any information storage and retrieval system, without permission in writing from the publisher.

Requests for permission to make copies of any part of the work should be addressed to School Permissions and Copyrights, Harcourt, Inc., 6277 Sea Harbor Drive, Orlando, Florida 32887-6777. Fax: 407-345-2418.

HARCOURT and the Harcourt Logo are trademarks of Harcourt, Inc., registered in the United States of America and/or other jurisdictions.

Printed in the United States of America

ISBN 10: 0-15-351086-2
ISBN 13: 978-0-15-351086-1

Ordering Options
ISBN 10: 0-15-350603-2 (Grade 6 On-Level Collection)
ISBN 13: 978-0-15-350603-1 (Grade 6 On-Level Collection)
ISBN 10: 0-15-357982-X (package of 5)
ISBN 13: 978-0-15-357982-0 (package of 5)

If you have received these materials as examination copies free of charge, Harcourt School Publishers retains title to the materials and they may not be resold. Resale of examination copies is strictly prohibited and is illegal.

Possession of this publication in print format does not entitle users to convert this publication, or any portion of it, into electronic format.

2 3 4 5 6 7 8 9 10   179   12 11 10 09 08 07

Susan Butcher took a deep breath and let out a silent plea. She didn't think she could wait much longer. Any minute now, they would call her number. In front of her, she could see her sled dogs, eager to begin running. Around her, the crowd watched and waited. Every two minutes, a new number was called. Then that musher's sled took off down the snowy trail.

The year was 1988. Susan was waiting her turn to begin the Iditarod. She and the other dogsled racers, or mushers, were about to set off on what many have dubbed "The Last Great Race on Earth."

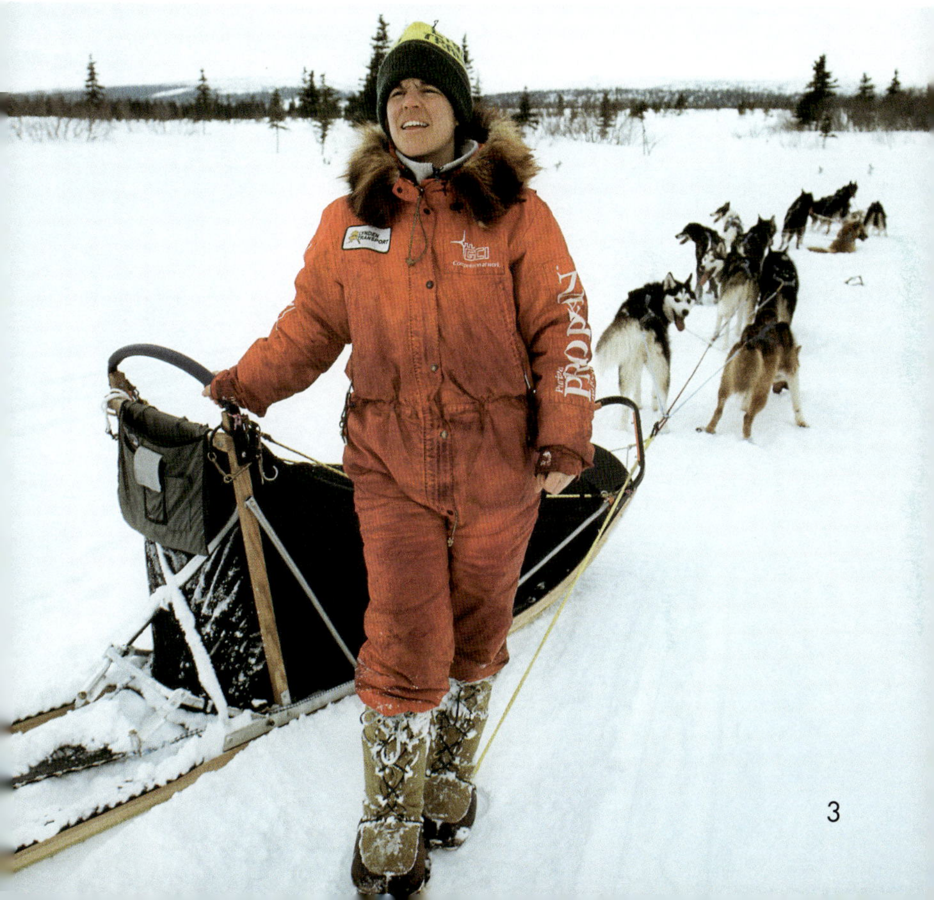

The Iditarod is a dogsled race between Anchorage and Nome, Alaska. The race trail covers over a thousand miles (1,868 km). It has taken place every year since 1973. The race was begun, in part, to honor a dogsled run that saved many lives in Nome in 1925. That's when twenty brave mushers rushed serum from Anchorage to Nome to save the people there from a lethal diptheria epidemic.

Many people feel that the Iditarod is the most challenging race in the world. It is certainly a difficult race. Mushers and their dog teams must guide 200-pound (90.7-kg) sleds up mountains and across streams. They must travel on sea ice and down frozen riverbeds. They have to deal with freezing temperatures, icy winds, and blizzards that make it almost impossible to see.

That's why Iditarod racers are a special sort. Most are determined people who love dogs and have lots of experience in the snow and cold.

That certainly described Susan. This was her eleventh Iditarod. She had been training and racing sled dogs for over fifteen years. More importantly, she had won the last two Iditarod races. Now she wanted to become a three-time champion. She wanted to do something that no one had ever done before. She wanted to win the Iditarod three years in a row. Some traditional old-timers still claimed that women weren't as good at dogsled racing as men. Susan wanted to put that idea to rest forever.

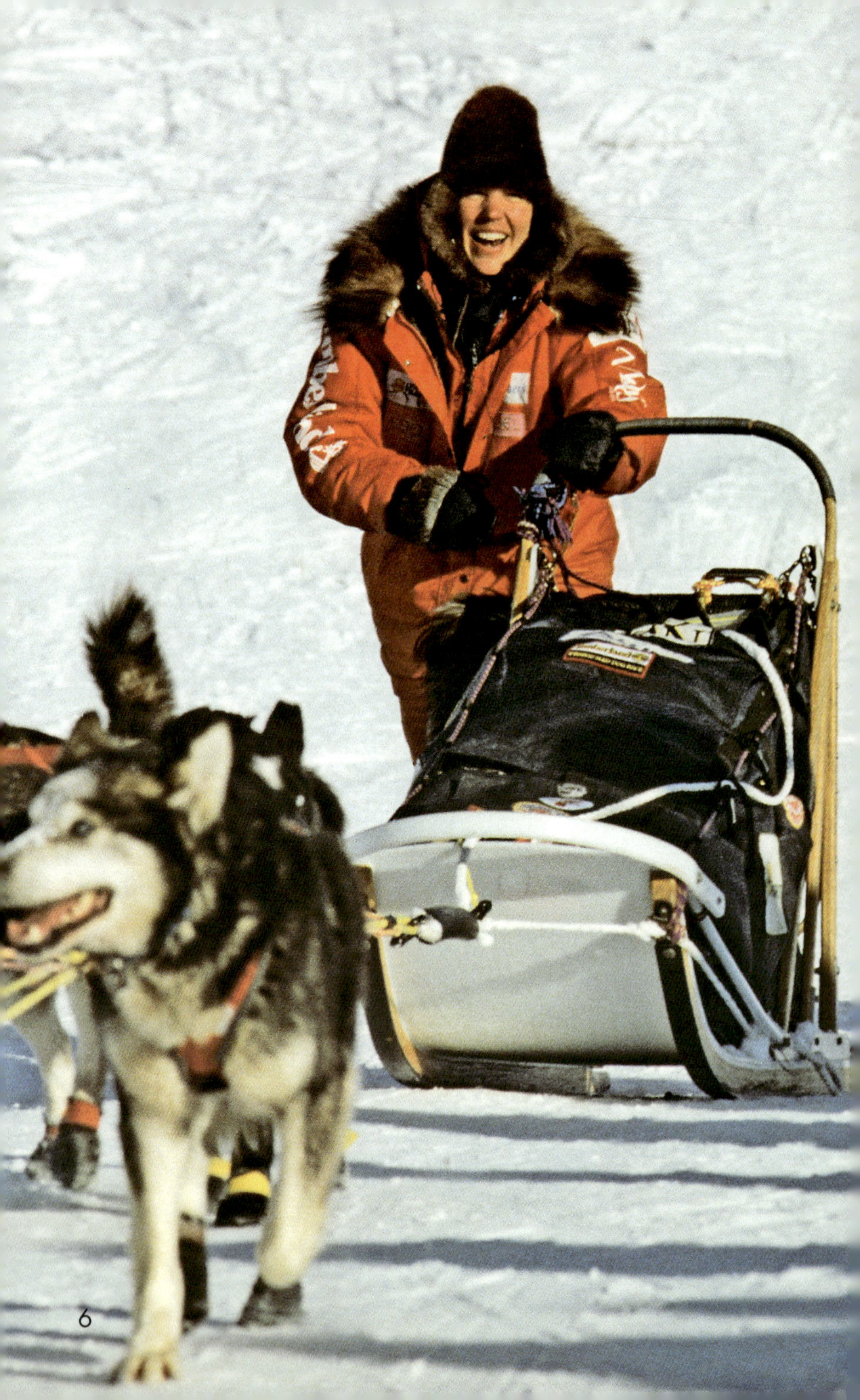

At last, Susan heard her number called. She moved to the starting line and cued her dogs. "All right!" she called. This told the dogs that it was time to run. In a flash, they were off. They wouldn't stop until they got to the first checkpoint at Eagle River, 20 miles (32 km) away.

Eagle River was only the first of twenty-four checkpoints on the 1,161-mile (1,868-km) trail. Susan knew the race would take about eleven days. The year before, she had set a record with her winning time of eleven days, two hours, five minutes, and thirteen seconds. She hoped to beat that time this year. However, she could never guess how things would turn out. The weather, and the possibility of accidents on the trail and dogs getting sick all conspired to make the race unpredictable. Of course, the unpredictability was one of the things Susan loved most about the Iditarod.

The previous year, for instance, something unpredictable and tragic had occurred. The first day on the trail, Jackie, one of her dogs, had suddenly keeled over, dead. An autopsy later showed that Jackie had had a liver problem that had never been diagnosed.

Still, Susan had persevered and won the race. After that, she felt that she could handle whatever this year's race had to dish out.

This year, the race started well. Susan breezed through the first three checkpoints. After that, it was a long run, 88 miles (142 km), to the next one. On this stretch of the trail, Susan kept her eyes out for moose. Moose were one of the few animal dangers that dog teams faced on the trail. Bears hibernated at this time of year, and there weren't many wolves around. Moose, however, could be deadly when they got hungry.

Susan knew that firsthand. In 1985, she had had a tragic encounter with a moose. The deep snow that covered the hillsides sometimes forced moose onto the trail. Susan had been on the lookout for moose as she drove her team along the trail. She knew that if she saw a moose, she would have to stop her dog team quickly. It was nighttime, and Susan was driving her sled by the light of a headlamp she wore. As she came up a hill, she saw her lead dog's ears perk up. Peering through the darkness, Susan tried to see what was wrong. Then, at the top of the hill, she saw it. A moose had stepped out onto the trail. It seemed crazed with hunger.

Susan tried desperately to stop her dogs before they got to the moose. Unfortunately, it was impossible. The moose ran into the team of harnessed dogs, attacking them. Susan waved an ax at the moose, but it wasn't scared away. It came after more of the dogs. Granite, Susan's brave lead dog, tried to intercept the moose before it could attack again. The moose slammed Granite into a tree.

Finally, another Iditarod racer showed up and shot the moose. However, two of Susan's dogs had been killed, and several others had been badly injured. Heartbroken, Susan dropped out of the race to care for her injured dogs.

Never a quitter, Susan returned the next year, and the year after that, to win the Iditarod. Now she wanted this year, 1988, to be another winning year as well. From the start, it looked as if things were going her way. She was making good time, stopping at the checkpoints, and continuing on her way.

At each checkpoint, she would first feed and tend to the dogs, and then rest a little herself as the dogs devoured their meal. As soon as she could, she would set off again, back on the trail. She wanted to make good time because she knew that there was a storm brewing.

Susan had already reached the coast when the storm hit. The coast was the most dangerous part of the trail for many mushers. The storms there could be brutal, and part of the trail led over the frozen, ice-covered sea.

Susan had been behind several other racers, but they had all decided to wait out the storm. That's when Susan made her bold decision. She would keep going through the storm. Her dogs knew the coast. She had often brought them here on training runs.

As she set out, the wind came in so hard that it almost knocked the dogs off of their feet. Susan wondered if her decision had been the right one. She had to stop every few minutes to wipe her dogs' frozen eyelashes. Several times, her sled turned over.

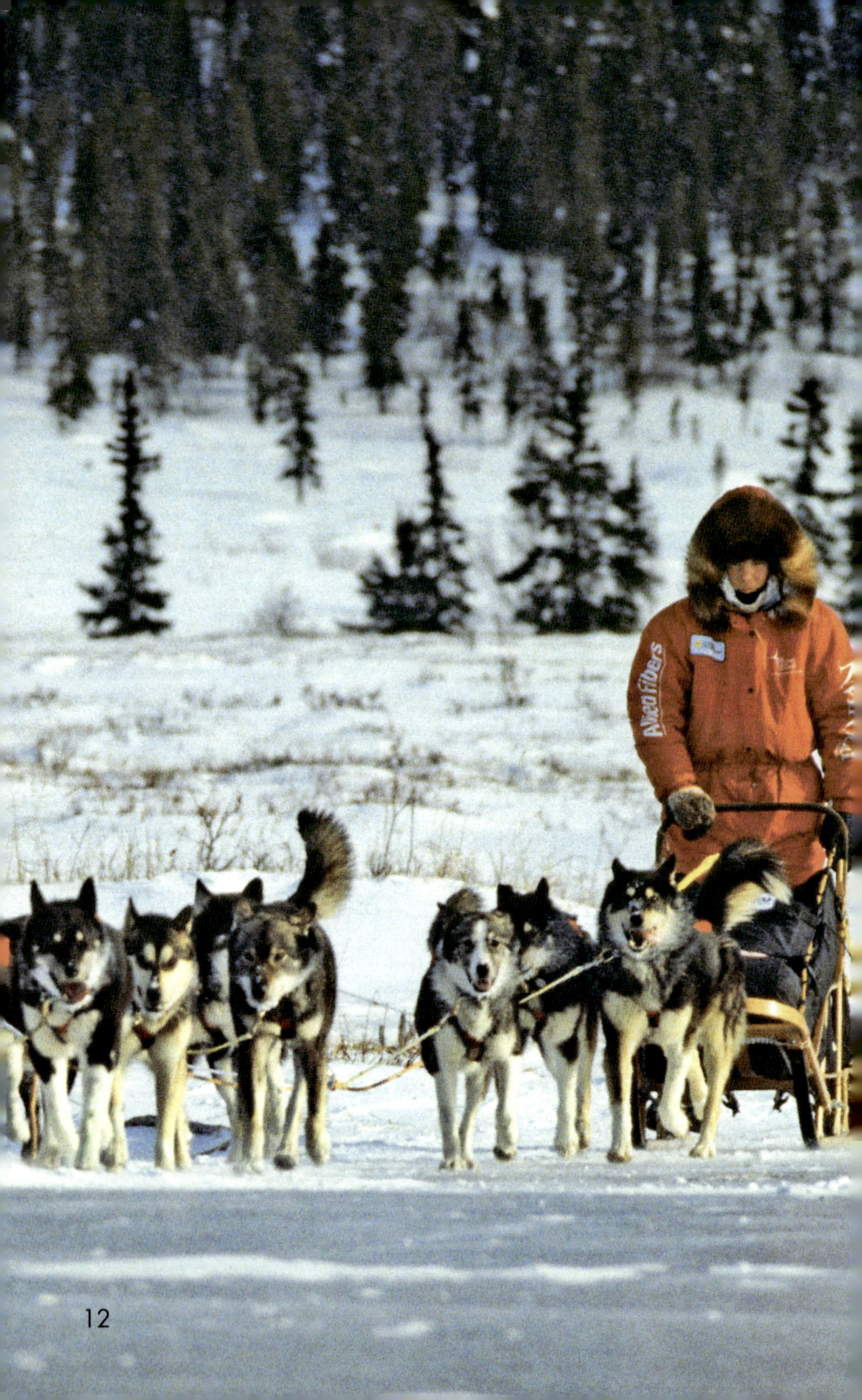

Worst of all was crossing the frozen sea. Susan had to be very careful where she drove the sled. One wrong move could land her and her dogs in icy water. It was one thing when a little water from a stream seeped into her clothes. However, falling into a hole in the ice was a completely different story. If she didn't drown, her wet clothes would almost certainly cause her to freeze to death.

Plus, the storm was so bad she wasn't sure where the sea ice ended and the ground began. If she went the wrong way, she could find herself stuck out at sea. The ice she was traveling on could break off and float away, taking her with it.

Susan thought back to another year's Iditarod. In 1984, she had been out on the sea ice when it had given way. Susan and the sled had fallen into the water. Fortunately, Granite and the rest of the sled dog team had pulled her out. Otherwise she would have drowned.

Even so, she had to be very careful for the rest of the race. She knew she needed to dry her clothes. This could be done by running along with the dogs, but if she ran too hard, her lungs would have frozen in the cold temperatures. On the other hand, if she rode in the sled, her clothes would have never dried, and she would have frozen to death. Practical as ever, Susan alternated running and riding. Her clothes dried, and she arrived in Nome in second place.

This year, Susan didn't want to repeat her icy dunking. She sighed in relief when she was finally sure she was off of the ice and back on land. The most treacherous part of the race was over. She was ahead of everyone else who had decided to wait out the storm.

Susan drove her sled down the trail quickly. She was headed for a rendezvous with victory at the finish line in Nome. She was about to make history.

As she arrived in the center of Nome, she could hear the cheers from the crowd. For the third time in three years, Susan Butcher had crossed the finish line first. She had set a record with three straight Iditarod wins!

Think Critically

1. What is the Iditarod?

2. How did Susan Butcher make history?

3. Summarize what happened to Susan during the 1985 Iditarod.

4. How can you tell that Susan is brave?

5. Would you ever want to race in the Iditarod? Why or why not?

Social Studies

Learn About Alaska Use the Internet or an encyclopedia to research some facts about Alaska for a travel brochure. Possible ideas to include are cities, animals, and natural wonders. Fold a piece of paper in thirds and create your brochure.

 School-Home Connection Tell family members about Susan Butcher and the Iditarod. Discuss what qualities you admire in a competitor like Susan.

Word Count: 1,516